COLOURFUL
Creation

Lucy Moore

Illustrated by Honor Ayres

Imagine a time there

No chairs and no tables, no carpets, no wall.
No houses, no cities, no flowers, no sun.
No books! No computers! This place was no fun!

was nothing at all.

It was all dank and dreary, and manky and lonely;
all over the surface of earth there was only
a shuddering, juddering, bubbling muddle of mud.

But hovering over this chaos...

...You guessed!
The Spirit of God, like a hen on a nest.
Watching and waiting in anticipation
until he would start his great work of creation.

'Let there be light!' a mighty voice called
and there in the dark shone the first light of all—
like the flick of a match, then it grew to a blaze
and it lit up the world like the smile on God's face.
God gently divided the dark from the light.
He called the one 'Day' and the other one 'Night'.
There was evening and morning—the very first day.

Once he'd begun he was well in his stride.
'Now let's have a glorious sky,' the Lord cried.

'We'll make it a paint pot of every colour
to stretch high and wide. Oh, it would be far duller
to have only earth!' Sky appeared with no trouble
protecting the world like a beautiful bubble.
There was evening and morning—the second day.

On day three the Lord rolled his sleeves up and said...

...'This earth is too soggy and boggy. Instead
we need somewhere to walk where we won't get wet feet.
You waters, roll back, please. Now this is quite neat.
We'll have something called "Land" and something called "Sea".
On the something called "Land" we'll grow something called "Tree".'

And God got excited. Instead of one tree,
he pictured the land how he'd like it to be.
He made the ground grow plants of all shapes and sizes,
from poplars to peonies, date palms to daisies.
Canadian Redwoods, strawberries, swede,
toadstools and tamarinds, spinach, seaweed,
rainforests, cacti and calm English woods.
God grinned when he saw it and said, 'Hmm, that's good!'

The next day
he looked up
and said,

'What we need...

...are some lights in the heavens above—yes, indeed!
We'll use them to mark out the days and the seasons
and months and the years. There are plenty of reasons
for setting a place for the moon and the sun,
And throwing in stars—oh, this is great fun!'

(Did he flick out his fingers to spatter the sun,
moon and stars through the sky? Or was every one
designed, built and painted with infinite care?
I don't know. Look up and decide, if you dare!)

On day five the Lord God,

he had the great notion...

...Of filling with life every lake, sea and ocean.
'We'll have big fish and small fish, and fat ones and skinny!
We'll make the seas teem with things floppy and finny!'

Yes! We'll have birds, too!

14

All diving and soaring...

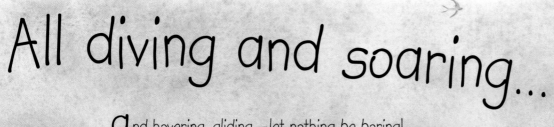

...and hovering, gliding—let nothing be boring!
And look! There were guppies and clownfish and whales,
ferocious sea monsters with sharp teeth and scales.

Penguins with short, and emus with long legs.
God sent them all off to lay hundreds of eggs.
'It's good, it's so good!' the birds heard him say.
There was evening and morning—that was the fifth day.

On day six, the Lord

went completely to town!

'**W**e'll have oodles of animals, some yellow, some brown.
We'll have a great range of things all fluffy and hairy.
Some cute and cuddly, some sleek and scary!

Reptiles! Marsupials! Amphibians! Mammals!
Cougars, koalas, chameleons and camels!
Terrapins, tree frogs, things ending in "saurus",
pandas, pigs, porcupines—it will be glorious!'

'But now,' said the Lord...

...When all this was done,

'I want someone with a heart after my own.

This world I have made, it needs looking after.

It needs gardening, farming and filling with laughter.

And so for the world here, my masterpiece
will be women and men who will rule birds and beasts,
and the flowers and plants and the trees and the fishes.
My people will take care of each unique species.

I hope they enjoy it. I hope they discover
that God, earth and humans were made for each other.'
So God made the people he loved and he blessed,
then put his feet up for a well-deserved rest.

19

Now you know that the earth
has been given to you
as a present to treasure...

...so what will you do?